TRAVL
COOKBOOK

AUTO, RV, AND SEMI MEALS MADE EASY

PATRICIA CHURCHEY

DENVER, COLORADO

Traveler's Cookbook
Auto, RV, and Semi Meals Made Easy

Outskirts Press, Inc.
http://www.outskirtspress.com

ISBN: 978-1-4787-7213-2

PRINTED IN THE UNITED STATES OF AMERICA

I wish to thank my Lord and Savior Jesus
for making this book possible.
I want to thank Him for all the great foods and
the wonderful protection
He's given me throughout the years of traveling our great nation.
Last but not forgotten, thanks to my brothers for field
testing these recipes on construction sites.

A list of things to have for cooking on the go. Having some basic but simple spices and utensils handy will make your meals easier to make.

Spices may include salt, pepper, garlic powder, and cloves. Meat tenderizer, or any other spices that you prefer.

Utensils may include a fork, spoon, and knife. I also find a slotted spoon, spatula (metal and plastic), ladle (gravy spoon), and a couple of sharp short-bladed knives can be handy for cutting veggies or meats.

I have a handheld can opener, aluminum foil, some aluminum loaf pans, and a box of oven bags, large size (five in the box).

I carry a small piece of board that I cover with foil to use as a cutting board. There are many ways to cook while traveling and many new gadgets to do so. But I will share the ones I've used over the years as an over-the-road driver with you. You can have a hot meal without ever taking a cooking class or paying a high price for eating out. I hope to help my fellow travelers to get that hot meal easily and without fuss.

So, to start, you may want to look at some basic items found in every truck stop or large mega store.

1. Find a power inverter (converter), 150 watts or more, that will plug into a 12-volt outlet.

2. Find a small (1 qt.) crock pot (100 watts) or a lunch box stove and some small plastic bowls with lids.

* Formula to figure watts is amps x volts = watts

On every appliance is a sticker with the amps and volts written on it.

Common Measures

CUP	FLUID OZ	TBSP	TSP	MILLILITER
1 C	8 Oz	16 Tbsp	48 Tsp	237 Ml
3/4 C	6 Oz	12 Tbsp	36 Tsp	177 Ml
2/3 C	5 Oz	11 Tbsp	32 Tsp	158 Ml
1/2 C	4 Oz	8 Tbsp	24 Tsp	118 Ml
1/3 C	3 Oz	5 Tbsp	16 Tsp	79 Ml
1/4 C	2 Oz	4 Tbsp	12 Tsp	59 Ml
1/8 C	1 Oz	2 Tbsp	6 Tsp	30 Ml
1/16 C	.5 Oz	1 Tbsp	3 Tsp	15 Ml

C = Cup
Oz = Ounces
Tbsp = Tablespoon
Tsp = Teaspoon
Ml = Milliliter

Table of Contents

CONTENTS

Baked Chicken

NEEDED:

- 1 raw chicken less than 3 lbs.
- Spices
- 1 small yellow apple
- ¼ cup water
- 1 oven bag
- Lunch box stove or crockpot
- Fork and large spoon
- Small bowl with a lid

Put the apple into the chicken. Sprinkle the spices over the chicken. Put the chicken into the cooker. Add the water to the chicken and cover and cook three hours on low. Turn off and let cool until you can touch the chicken. Remove the chicken from the bag and turn it over to cook another three hours. The chicken is done when you pull on the leg and only have a bone in your fingers. You can make chicken sandwiches or use the chicken for other dishes. Store the leftovers in the small bowl. Eat and enjoy.

Baked Potatoes

NEEDED:

- Small potatoes (so they fit in your hand closed), red skin or white skin
- Crockpot or lunch box stove
- ¼ cup water
- Aluminum foil

Place potatoes in cooker; add water (cook on high). Put aluminum foil over them. Cook on low for thirty minutes and turn potatoes. Cook another thirty minutes. They are done when you can push a fork into them easily.

*You can cook potatoes in a microwave. Just put holes in them all around with a fork and cook three to five minutes (on high) until you can push the fork into them easily. Sit, eat, and enjoy.

BBQ Chicken, BBQ Beef, BBQ Pork

NEEDED:

- 1 lb of chicken, beef, or pork
- BBQ sauce (your choice)
- Spices: your choice
- 1 oven bag
- ¼ cup water
- Crockpot or lunch box stove

Put the meat and spices into the oven bag. Put the bag into the cooker add the water. Cook on low until meat is tender and falling apart, about two hours. Remove the meat and drain out excess liquid from the bag. Do not put a hole in the bag. Put the bag into the cooker add the meat and pour in the BBQ sauce a little at a time. Stir the meat and get it covered by the sauce; cook another hour. Then sit, eat, and enjoy.

Beef Heart with Baked Potatoes

NEEDED:

- 1 to 2 lb. piece of beef heart, raw
- Meat tenderizer and spices
- 3 or 4 small potatoes
- 1 small onion
- ¼ cup of water
- Fork and knife
- 1 oven bag
- Crockpot or lunch box oven

Using the knife, stab holes in to the piece of heart all over it. Sprinkle the meat tenderizer and spices on it. Put the oven bag in to the cooker. Add the water and the meat. Peel and cut into four pieces the onion and put in the meat. Cover it and cook it about four to five hours on low. The meat is done when it's easy to cut. Pick up the bag and place the potatoes under it; cook for another hour. The potatoes are done when the fork goes into them easily. Sit back, eat, and enjoy.

Beef Mac and Cheese

NEEDED:

- Crockpot or lunch box stove
- 1 lb. ground beef or turkey
- Oven bag
- 1 can premade mac and cheese
- Fork or spoon

Cook meat until done, stirring often to keep from sticking.

Add premade mac and cheese, heat for one hour. Eat and enjoy.

Beef Stew

NEEDED:

- Lunch box stove or Crockpot
- Oven bag
- 1 to 2 lbs. Beef (steak or roast, etc., cut into small cubes)
- Black pepper
- Meat tenderizer
- Spray margarine
- Fresh mixed veggies or frozen mixed veggies or canned veggies

Place the beef in to the oven bag, spray on the margarine, sprinkle on pepper and meat tenderizer. Place the oven bag in the cooker and cook one hour. Then turn over the meat and cook for thirty minutes. Then add veggies, cook another hour, and then eat.

*Using the crockpot, cook on low.

Buffalo Wings

NEEDED:

- Lunch box stove
  Crockpot
- Oven bag
- 6 to 9 Chicken wings
- BBQ sauce
- Hot sauce (if you like it)
- Aluminum foil

Place chicken wings in an oven bag. Place the bag in oven; cook about one and a half hours. Line the oven with foil and put a small amount of BBQ sauce in the oven. Lay wings on the sauce and cover with more sauce; cook another forty-five minutes to one hour and eat.

*Cook the wings in the crock pot, put the wings in to a clean oven bag and cover with BBQ sauce; cook on low for one hour uncovered.

Chicken and Rice

NEEDED:

- Crockpot or lunch box stove
- Oven bag
- 1 to 3 lbs. of chicken
- Instant rice (bag)
- Spices
- Fork or spoon
- Water

Put chicken into oven bag. Place this into crockpot or stove. Cover with water and add spices. Cook one to three hours; if the chicken falls off the leg bone easily, it's done. You can remove the chicken, cool it, and remove the bones. Add another cup of water; pour a bag of instant rice in to the oven bag. Cook one hour and enjoy.

Chicken and Vegetable Soup

- 2 raw chicken breasts or 4 raw chicken legs or 4 raw thighs
- Spices: whatever you want
- ¼ cup of water
- 1 oven bag
- Crockpot or lunch box stove
- 1 lb bag of frozen vegetables (your choice)

Put the chicken into the oven bag. Place the bag into your cooker; add the spices and the water. Cook on low until the chicken falls off the bone (approximately two hours) Remove the bones, skin, etc, from the bag and add the vegetables. Cook approximately one hour until vegetables are soft. If you want more broth to add crackers, add more water and cook for another half an hour. Sit, eat, and enjoy.

Chicken Vegetable Stir-Fry

NEEDED:

- Leftover baked chicken or prepackaged chicken strips 8 oz. to 1 lb.
- 1 package frozen stir-fry vegetables 16 oz.
- 3 Tbsps margarine
- 1 oven bag
- Lunch box stove or crockpot

Place margarine and chicken into oven bag, put into cooker. Brown the chicken (cook on low) about thirty minutes. Add the vegetables; cook about forty minutes until soft. Eat and enjoy.

Chili

NEEDED:

- Lunch box oven or Crockpot
- Oven bag
- 1 lb ground chuck or 1 lb ground turkey or 1 lb ground beef
- 15oz can stewed tomatoes with green chilies
- Beans (your choice) 2 cans 15 oz.
- Chili powder and other spices (your choice)

Place meat in the bag, then into the oven. Cook a half an hour. Then stir the meat, so it can cook evenly. Cook another half hour. Now add the spices and drain the tomatoes and add to the bag. Cook another hour; then add the beans and cook two hours or more. Then eat.

*Cook on low in the crockpot.

Corn on the Cob

NEEDED:

- 1–2 ears of corn
- Margarine
- Oven bag
- Lunch box stove or crockpot

Pull husks off of the ears. Cover with margarine. Put them in the bag and put into the cooker. To put into the crockpot, break them in half. Cook on low, rolling them around every five to ten minutes. Cook for about thirty minutes. When the fork goes into the kernel easily, it's done. Enjoy.

*The corn can be placed in an inside-out plastic shopping bag and cooked in the microwave three minutes for one ear. Two ears take five minutes, rolling them once during cooking.

Gizzards

NEEDED:

- 1 to 2 lb. Gizzards
- Lunch box oven
- Oven bag
- Black pepper
- Meat tenderizer
- Garlic powder

Place gizzards in bag; put on pepper, etc. Place the bag in the oven, cook about one hour, and then turn and cook another hour. These are best when hot.

*Cook on low in the crockpot.

Hot Ham and Cheese Sandwiches

NEEDED:

- Lunch box stove
- Aluminum foil
- Fork

Place a piece of foil in the bottom of the stove (cover the bottom). Place the ham slice on it and cook about five minutes; then turn it over for another five minutes. Place cheese on the ham and close the lid for about thirty seconds, until the cheese melts. You can steam the bread as for hot dogs or put the ham and cheese on bread and enjoy.

This recipe can be used in the crockpot as well.

Hamburgers

NEEDED:

- 1 lb. hamburger or ground turkey
- Spices: your choice
- Aluminum foil
- Crockpot or lunch box stove
- Plastic spatula

Pat out your burgers to fit the appliance you're using. Put your spices on the meat. Line the bottom of the appliance with the aluminum foil. Cook the meat on high, turning the meat over about every fifteen to twenty minutes. Cook until they are done. Fully cooked takes about fifty-five minutes. You can top with cheese slices or shredded cheese for cheeseburgers. Sit back, eat, and enjoy.

Hot Dogs

- Lunch box stove
- Aluminum foil
- Fork
- Hot dogs

Tear off a piece of foil larger than the bottom of the stove. Line the bottom of the stove with the foil. Place the hot dogs on the foil and turn on the stove. Wait for five minutes and roll the dogs around the stove; do this as often as needed until done (about ten minutes). To heat the buns, lift a corner of the foil with a fork, add a small amount of water, place the buns on the dogs, and close the stove for about two minutes.

This recipe can be used with the crockpot, but the dogs may be cut in half before cooking.

Pork and Sauerkraut

NEEDED:

- Lunch box oven or
- Crockpot
- Oven bag
- 1 to 2 lb. Pork
- Meat tenderizer
- Black pepper

Place pork in oven bag; add meat tenderizer and black pepper. Put in oven and cook one hour; then turn over and cook for another hour. Then add sauerkraut, cook one hour, and eat.

Above is cooked in lunch box oven; when cooking in a crockpot, set temp on low to cook.

Pork Tenderloin

NEEDED:

- Crockpot or lunch box stove
- Oven bag
- Pork tenderloin (plain or seasoned)
- Fork or 2 large spoons to remove it after cooking
- Aluminum foil
- Water

Put the tenderloin on to cook. Cook for three to four hours. It's done when the meat falls apart easily. Put on aluminum foil and cut to serve.

Quick and Easy Meaty Salad

NEEDED:

- 1 premade salad (from a grocery store or truck stop)
- 1 package tuna or precooked chicken strips
- 1 bottle of salad dressing (your choice)
- Paper bowl
- Spoon/fork

Open the meat package and add meat to the salad. Add the dressing. Eat and enjoy.

Rice and Beans

NEEDED:

- Crockpot or lunch box oven
- Can opener
- Knife or scissors
- Fork
- Oven bag
- 1 or 2 cans of beans (your choice)
- Boil in bag of rice (instant, white, or brown)

Put the bag into the crockpot or stove. Put the rice in it; cover with water about one knuckle over the rice.

Cook until the rice is done (about fifty minutes).

Remove rice bag; be careful—it's very hot. You can use a fork to pull it up; then cut it open and pour it into the bag. Open the beans, add to rice, stir, and add spices if you want. Cook for another hour and eat.

Sausage Perlow

NEEDED:

- 1 lb. package beef or turkey sausage link
- 1 small onion (hand size)
- Spices: whatever you want
- 3 Tbsp (tablespoons) margarine
- 15 oz. can stewed tomatoes with chilies (mild or hot)
- 2 ½ cups water
- 1 cup of instant rice
- Can opener
- Large spoon
- 1 oven bag
- Crockpot or lunch box oven

Cut the sausage in small pieces like coins, about ½ inch thick. Peel the onion and dice (cut into small pieces). Put the margarine into the oven bag with the sausage and onions. Cook on low for about thirty minutes, stirring often (until it's brown). Then open the can of tomatoes; pour off the liquid. Put tomatoes and spices in to cooker. Add the water and turn on to high. After about thirty minutes, stir and add the rice. Stir slowly as you add it. Cover it and cook for approximately forty minutes. If the rice is soft, the food is done. Sit back, eat, and enjoy.

Smoked Meats and Beans

NEEDED:

- 3 or 4 smoked pork neck bones or 2 ham hocks
- 2 or 3 cans of beans (your choice) or black-eyed peas
- 1 can opener
- 1 oven bag
- 1 large spoon
- Crockpot or lunch box stove
- ¼ cup water

Place meat into oven bag. Put into cooker; add the water. Cook on low for about three to four hours, until meat is soft and comes off the bone easily. Remove the bones and fat. Add the beans or black-eyed peas to the meat and cook for two more hours. Stir every thirty minutes. * Note: You can add about half a cup of instant rice during the last two hours, if you want it. Sit back, eat, and enjoy.

Squash and Onions

NEEDED:

- 6–8 yellow squash
- 1 small yellow onion
- ¼ cup water
- Salt/pepper
- 1 oven bag
- Crockpot or lunch box oven

Slice the squash into coin-like pieces about half an inch thick. Put them into the bag add the water and the salt and pepper and the diced onion. Cook until tender about three hours, stirring once or twice. Enjoy.

* These can be cooked in the microwave three to seven minutes.

Stuffed Pork Chops

NEEDED:

- 1 pork chop cut 1 ½ to 2 inches thick, with a pocket for stuffing

  The pork chops can be found at a grocery store with the stuffing in them.
- 1 oven bag
- Lunch box stove or crockpot
- ¼ cup of water

Put the oven bag in the cooker. Place the pork chop in it; add the water. Cook for thirty minutes. Turn the chop over and cook on the other side. It will be done when you cut it and the meat is white all the way through. Sit, eat, and enjoy.

Turkey Breast and Mashed Potatoes

NEEDED:

- 1 turkey breast
- 1 pack instant potatoes (4.1 oz./4-1/2 cup servings)
- Crockpot
- Or lunch box stove
- 1 oven bag
- Paper plates or paper bowls
- Utensils

Put the turkey breast in the oven bag and put into the cooker. Cook for approximately three hours on low until it falls apart when touched with a fork. Move the turkey to a bowl or plate. Add the instant potatoes to the leftover drippings from the turkey and stir. Sit, eat, and enjoy.

9 781478 772132